The Forever Fight:
ON DRUGS, ALCOHOL, AND THE CYCLE OF ADDICTION

By: K.J. GORDON

Source: National Institute on Drug Abuse
National Institute of Health
U.S. Department of Health and Human Services

Copyright © 2016 by K.J. Gordon

All rights reserved. No part of this publication may be reproduced, distributed, or transmitted in any form or by any means, including photocopying, recording, or other electronic or mechanical methods, without the prior written permission of the publisher, except in the case of brief quotations embodied in critical reviews and certain other noncommercial uses permitted by copyright law. For permission requests, write to the publisher, addressed "Attention: Permissions Coordinator," at the address below.

5D Media Publishing
35 W 31st Street
New York, NY 10001
www.5Dmedia.org

Ordering Information:
Quantity sales. Special discounts are available on quantity purchases by corporations, associations, and others. For details, contact the publisher at the address above.

Orders by U.S. trade bookstores and wholesalers. Please contact Big Distribution: Tel: **(212) 537-7177; Fax: (800) 778-4872** or visit www.5DMedia.org.

Printed in the United States of America

The Forever Fight on Drugs, Alcohol, and the Cycle of Addiction / K.J. Gordon

ISBN-10: 0-9989217-0-X
ISBN-13: 978-0-9989217-0-9

First Edition

DEDICATION

For those in the fight –
The ones suffering with an addiction
& the ones who care

CONTENTS

Acknowledgments   1

PART I
On Drugs & Alcohol

Introduction	5
Why People Use Drugs	9
Methamphetamine	13
Heroin	17
Marijuana	21
Cocaine	31
Alcohol	35
Prescription Drugs	41

PART II
On Addiction & Recovery

Identifying a Drug Problem	57
Signs of Addiction in Others	69
How Addiction Works	75
Addiction Recovery	83
Safe Detoxing	97
Working the 12 Steps	105
Building Your Self Esteem	111
Involving the Family	117
Interventions	123
The Cycle of Addiction	129
The Forever Fight	135

ACKNOWLEDGMENTS

To those feeling trapped in this fight - Stress, loss, pain, and pressure from others may make you feel like there's no way out. If you want out, but the struggle is calling you to use or to relapse, remind yourself that YOU DESERVE BETTER!

When you have had enough of living with your addiction, know that there are people who care. A Conversation could go a long way. Understand that you are one amongst millions of people suffering with addiction that feels powerless over drugs or alcohol. You have a choice to give in to your addiction, or to get help and CHOOSE LIFE! To speak to someone who cares, and has been there before, call **1(844)775-HELP** (4357).

K. J. Gordon

PART I

ON DRUGS & ALCOHOL

THE FOREVER FIGHT

K. J. Gordon

CHAPTER 1

INTRODUCTION

Life is often underestimated and treated as a simple game that can be won by playing by a certain set of rules. But, in the game of life there are ongoing rule changes and game inequalities. Life is hard. It can be crazy, and stressful, and often unfair.

The realization of the reality of one's life and life circumstances can be difficult to face. To cope, some people numb their emotions with whatever they feel will be the most affective - from conversations with a professional, to dedication to religion, to drug or alcohol use, in an attempt to numb the pain these feelings cause.

Drug and alcohol use has been a popular go to for centuries. As the availability and strength of these numbing agents increase, the dependence on them grows. There are various reasons someone would begin a dependence on these substances. All users are looking for a form of escape from a physical or mental pain or emotion, to temporarily change how they feel.

In 2013, an estimated 24.6 million Americans age 12 and over, 9.4 percent of the population, had used an illicit drug in the past month. This number is up from 8.3 percent in 2002. This increase was primarily due to a rise in marijuana use, the most commonly used prescribed drug.

Statistics reveal that drug and alcohol abuse is now beginning earlier in life, with most people using drugs for the first time when they are teenagers. There were just over 2.8 million new users of non-prescribed drugs in 2013, or about 7,800 new users per day. Over half (54.1 percent) were under 18 years of age.

More than half of new illicit drug users begin with marijuana. The next most common being prescription pain relievers, followed by inhalants (which is most common amongst younger teens).

Although drug use and abuse are often used to soothe emotion or physical pain, the resulting health effects are the most detrimental to the human body. Drug addiction is the single ailment that spans across race, as well as economic and social classes. This includes everyone, from celebrities, professional athletes, suburban housewife's, to CEOs.

THE FOREVER FIGHT

If you find yourself or a loved one struggling with a dependence to drugs or alcohol, what can you do? The answer is – a lot. If you find yourself with a problem, the time to take action is now. Once you realize you have a problem, you can get help. You can check yourself into a rehabilitation facility, or try to take action on your own or with the help of loved ones.

This book is a step towards that help. It is intended for those suffering from addiction - the addict and their loved ones. We will review everything from why people use drugs and alcohol and to signs of a problem, to addressing the various drugs that are most likely to cause dependence. We have also outlined strategies suggested by experts that can help you get on track to living a drug-free life.

If you are reading this because you are suffering and have already identified that you have a problem, decide NOW that you do not want to be addicted any longer. You are more than an "Addict"! Please understand that only YOU can overcome your dependence on drugs or alcohol. Start your journey toward recovery today. It won't be easy, but you can do it.

CHAPTER 2

WHY PEOPLE USE DRUGS

Drugs help people. They ease the feeling of physical pain from an injury, as well as the feeling of emotional pain caused by losing a loved one or a personal tragedy. Drugs are drugs, whether they are prescribed by a medical professional, or made in a home kitchen from household items. Our bodies are made up of electrical impulses and chemical reactions. When drugs or alcohol enter the body, the chemistry is altered, and everything is affected in one way the other.

Prescription drugs are regulated and tested by medical experts who prescribe strength and dosage amounts based on how they will effect a patient's entire body. When people self-medicate, without taking all other factors into consideration, the consequences can be devastating. The drugs may "help" with one thing, while destroying internal organs and altering the chemical balances inside the body.

People use drugs for various reasons, but all are expecting the same result - a feeling of euphoria that makes them feel better, at least temporarily. We all want "happiness." A central driver in mood and motivation for "pleasure" is a chemical inside your body called Dopamine.

The Dopamine levels in your brain can be seen as a type of pleasure meter. Let's say your body can naturally produce 100 percent Dopamine levels, on its natural scale of 1-100. When you are happy, your levels increase towards that 100 percent. People are motivated to perform behaviors that will increase Dopamine levels as frequently as possible. We eat our favorite foods to increase Dopamine, spend time with people we love to increase Dopamine, and engage in extracurricular activities to increase Dopamine. When new substances like drugs or alcohol enter the body, one chemical change that occurs is a false increase of Dopamine to, let's say, 150 percent, and an expansion of your perceived "pleasure" scale to 1-150. Consequently, when you are not high on the drugs, the highest "pleasure" level you can achieve remains at 100.

By tricking your brain into thinking it is happiest when using drugs or alcohol by falsely inflating Dopamine levels, you will have more perceived "pleasure" when using than when not. When this part of the brain - which controls an individual's reward, motivation, learning, memory, and behavior - are altered in this way, addiction is born.

There are hundreds of ways that drugs are used as coping mechanisms, and each person has their own reason why they choose to use a certain drug. They can help calm you down, give you energy, overcome shyness, and avoid feelings of loneliness. Drugs may make you feel bolder and want to take risks you wouldn't normally take. They are used to perhaps fit into social situation and get into a "party" mood, and even to celebrate happy occasions. They are also used as a response to peer pressure, when someone wants to fit in, feel included, or experience for themselves what others have.

Medically, drugs are used to alleviate pain, help you to sleep, suppress anger, combat anxiety, and avoid depression. They can be used to cope with stress, stimulate your desire for sex, and lose weight.

The ways drugs affect us are countless—for everyone. So much so, that often it seems as if drugs can cure all our ills and help us overcome whatever bothers us. If that was all there were to it, we might consider each drug to be some kind of special "wonder drug".

A false sense of comfort is brought on by drugs, making users comfortable, pain free, and feel as if all of life problems are solved. A user's body begins to crave this feeling of euphoria, and gravitate to how it feels when using drugs. This is when it becomes a problem. The body craves a feeling of increased Dopamine levels that it cannot achieve on its own, leading the brain to convince itself that the body on drugs or alcohol is its new normal. Your body becomes physically hooked and dependent on these substances.

Instead of coping with life, drugs are used to distort reality, causing a vicious cycle. Users mentally feel as if they cannot live without the feelings that drugs give them, and that they just won't be able to cope with life without those drugs. This mental and physical state of dependence is when addiction is born.

Let's look at various illicit drugs that have a high rate of abuse, and see how each impacts the user.

CHAPTER 3

METHAMPHETAMINE

Methamphetamine use is on the rise. A rapid spread has occurred throughout the United States, mainly because it is manmade and easy to produce using common household items. Popularly known as Meth, it is often referred to as speed, chalk, ice, crystal, and glass. It is taken orally, intra-nasally (snorting the powder), by needle injection, or by smoking. Abusers may become addicted quickly, needing higher volume doses and more frequent use.

Meth is a scary drug with horrible health implications. It is a highly addictive stimulant that is closely related to the prescription drug Amphetamine, but has longer lasting and more toxic effects on the brain and spinal cord. At comparable doses, much greater amounts of the drug get into the brain, making it a more potent stimulant than recommended by medical professionals.

Meth use increases wakefulness and physical activity, while decreasing ones' appetite. It increases the release of very high levels of dopamine, which stimulates brain cells, enhancing mood and body movement.

Taking even small amounts of methamphetamine can result in increased breathing, rapid heart rate, irregular heartbeat, increased blood pressure, and hyperthermia. Other effects of methamphetamine abuse may include irritability, anxiety, insomnia, confusion, tremors, convulsions, cardiovascular collapse and death.

Chronic, long-term use can lead to psychotic behavior, hallucinations, and strokes. People who use meth often cannot sleep – sometimes for days on end. They lose weight quickly because they do not eat. Meth addicts often lose teeth, look emaciated, and create sores on their bodies by scratching due to having built up nervous energy they are trying to get rid of.

Chronic methamphetamine abuse also significantly changes how the brain functions. By rapidly increasing the dopamine levels in the brain, Meth use gives users a "rush" or "flash" of euphoria with use. This feeling of "happiness" can easily lead to addiction. These chemical changes are associated with reduced motor speed and impaired verbal learning. Recent studies in chronic methamphetamine abusers have also revealed severe structural and functional changes in areas of the brain associated with emotion and memory, which may account for many of the emotional and cognitive problems observed in chronic methamphetamine abusers.

As we've already indicated, long-term effects may include paranoia, aggressiveness, extreme anorexia, memory loss, visual and auditory hallucinations, delusions, and severe dental problems.

Also, transmission of HIV and hepatitis B and C can be a consequence of methamphetamine abuse. Among abusers who inject the drug, infection with HIV and other infectious diseases is spread mainly through the re-use of contaminated syringes, needles, and other injection equipment by more than one person.

Beyond its devastating effects on individual health, methamphetamine abuse threatens whole communities, causing increasing crime rates, unemployment, child neglect or abuse, and other social issues.

K. J. Gordon

CHAPTER 4

HEROIN

Heroin is another drug that is becoming more prevalent in the United States. This may be in part due to a popular shift from abuse of prescription pain relievers to heroin, as it is a more accessible, cheaper alternative to obtain the same high. Processed from morphine usually into a white or brown powder, heroin is also known by many other names including smack, H, ska, and junk. It is estimated that about 23 percent of individuals who use heroin become dependent on it.

Heroin abuse is associated with serious health conditions, including fatal overdose, spontaneous abortion, collapsed veins, and, particularly in users who inject the drug, infectious diseases, including HIV/AIDS and hepatitis.

The short-term effects of heroin abuse appear soon after a single dose and disappear in a few hours. After an injection of heroin, the users feel a "rush" of euphoria, a warm flushing of the skin, a dry mouth, and heaviness in their arms and legs.

Following the initial euphoria, users enter a wakeful and drowsy state known as "on the nod." Mental functioning also becomes clouded due to the depression of the central nervous system. Heroin overdoses frequently involve a suppression of breathing

Long-term effects of heroin appear after repeated use for some period of time. Street heroin often contains toxic contaminants or additives that can clog blood vessels, causing permanent damage to the lungs, liver, kidneys or brain. Chronic users may develop collapsed veins, infection of the heart lining and valves, abscesses, cellulitis, and liver disease. Pulmonary complications, including various types of pneumonia, may result from the poor health of the abuser, as well as from heroin's depressing effects on ones breathing.

With regular heroin use, a tolerance develops, causing an abuser to need to use more to achieve the same high. As higher doses are used over time, the body adapts to the drugs being present inside the body. The body is then physical dependent, and withdrawal symptoms may occur if use is reduced or stopped. When a frequent heroin abuser attempts to stop using, at times as early as a few hours after the last administration, they experience drug cravings, restlessness, muscle and bone pain, insomnia, diarrhea and vomiting, cold flashes with goose bumps ("cold turkey"), kicking movements ("kicking the habit"), and other symptoms.

Major withdrawal symptoms peak between 48 and 72 hours after the last dose and subside after about a week. Sudden withdrawal by heavily dependent users who are in poor health is occasionally fatal, although heroin withdrawal is considered less dangerous than alcohol or barbiturate withdrawal by longtime abusers.

K. J. Gordon

CHAPTER 5

MARIJUANA

Many would argue that marijuana is not a harmful drug and that it should be as legal to buy and use as alcohol. Marijuana is the most commonly used illicit drug in the United States. The legalization of marijuana for medical use or adult recreation is now occurring at the state level. Second to alcohol, marijuana is the most commonly used drug by minors.

Marijuana is a dry, shredded green/brown mix of flowers, stems, seeds, and leaves of the hemp plant Cannabis Sativa. It usually is smoked as a cigarette (joint, nail), or in a pipe (bong). It also is smoked in blunts, which are cigars that have been emptied of tobacco and refilled with marijuana, often in combination with another drug. It can also be mixed in food or brewed as a tea.

As a more concentrated, resinous form it is called hashish and, as a sticky black liquid, hash oil. Marijuana smoke has a pungent and distinctive, usually sweet-and-sour odor. Some people think that the smoke smells like burning rope.

There are countless street terms for marijuana including pot, herb, weed, grass, widow, ganja, and hash, as well as terms derived from trademarked varieties of cannabis, such as Bubble Gum, Northern Lights, Fruity Juice, Afghani #1, and a number of Skunk varieties.

The main active chemical in marijuana is THC (delta-9-tetrahydrocannabinol). The membranes of certain nerve cells in the brain contain protein receptors that bind to THC. Once securely in place, THC kicks off a series of cellular reactions that ultimately lead to the high that users experience when they smoke marijuana.

When exhaled, THC in the marijuana quickly enters the bloodstream, and spreads throughout the body. It connects to cannabinoid receptors on nerve cells in the brain and influences a person's pleasure, memory, thought, concentration, sensory and time perception, and coordinated movement. As with all drugs, marijuana helps users accomplish a targeted physical or emotional state. There are numerous chemicals inside the marijuana plant, all triggering different responses in the body.

M*edical marijuana* refers to treating a disease or

symptom with the whole unprocessed marijuana plant or its basic extracts. There is growing interest in the marijuana chemical *cannabidiol* (CBD) to treat certain conditions such as childhood epilepsy, a disorder that causes a child to have violent seizures. Therefore, scientists have been specially breeding marijuana plants and making CBD in oil form for treatment purposes. As CBD is a cannabinoid that does not affect the mind or behavior, these drugs may be less desirable to recreational users because they are not intoxicating. It may be useful in reducing pain and inflammation, controlling epileptic seizures, and possibly even treating mental illness and addictions to other drugs.

As THC increases appetite and reduces nausea, the FDA-approved THC-based medications are used for these purposes. THC may also decrease pain, inflammation (swelling and redness), and muscle control problems.

Although many are using for medical reasons, most users, however, self-medicate with marijuana, and do not weigh its benefits against its consequences. They are chasing an intoxicating effect, and would not be interested in the above mentioned Medical Grade forms. There are risks to taking any drug. But, patients prescribed Medical

Marijuana do so under supervision and advisement of a medical professional. They understand the benefits and dosage ideals for their bodies, and have weighed them against the side effects. Those who self-medicate, often do not.

The short-term effects of marijuana can include problems with memory and learning; distorted perception; difficulty in thinking and problem solving; loss of coordination; an increased heart rate. Long term marijuana causes changes to the brain similar to other major drugs.

In addition to inflating dopamine levels, Marijuana use can have an adverse effect on the heart. One study has indicated that an abuser's risk of heart attack more than quadruples in the first hour after smoking marijuana. The researchers suggest that such an effect might occur from marijuana's effects on blood pressure and heart rate and reduced oxygen-carrying capacity of blood. A user's lungs are also affected.

Even infrequent use can cause burning and stinging of the mouth and throat, and a heavy cough. A frequent marijuana smoker may have many of the same respiratory problems as tobacco smokers, such as daily cough and phlegm production, more frequent acute chest illness, a heightened risk of lung infections, and a greater tendency to obstructed airways.

Smoking marijuana possibly increases the likelihood of developing cancer of the head or neck. Marijuana abuse also has the potential to promote cancer of the lungs and other parts of the respiratory tract because it contains irritants and carcinogens. In fact, marijuana smoke contains 50 to 70 percent more carcinogenic hydrocarbons than tobacco smoke. It also induces high levels of an enzyme that converts certain hydrocarbons into their carcinogenic form—levels that may accelerate the changes that ultimately produce malignant, or cancerous, cells.

Marijuana users usually inhale more deeply and hold their breath longer than tobacco smokers do, which increases the lungs' exposure to carcinogenic smoke. These facts suggest that, puff for puff, smoking marijuana may be more harmful to the lungs than smoking tobacco.

THC also impairs the immune system's ability to fight disease, leading to increased health issues in frequent marijuana users. In laboratory experiments that exposed animal and human cells to THC or other marijuana ingredients, the normal disease-preventing reactions of many of the key types of immune cells were inhibited. In other studies, mice exposed to THC or related substances were more likely than unexposed mice to develop bacterial infections and tumors.

Research clearly demonstrates that marijuana has the potential to cause problems in daily life or make a person's existing problems worse. Depression, anxiety, and personality disturbances have been associated with chronic marijuana use. Because marijuana compromises the ability to learn and remember information, the more a person uses marijuana the more he or she is likely to fall behind in accumulating intellectual, job, or social skills. Research has shown that marijuana's adverse impact on memory and learning can last for days or weeks after the acute effects of the drug wear off. Students who smoke marijuana get lower grades and are less likely to graduate from high school, compared with their nonsmoking peers.

These "heavy" marijuana abusers had more trouble sustaining and shifting their attention, and in registering, organizing, and using information than did the study participants who had abused marijuana no more than 3 of the previous 30 days. As a result, someone who smokes marijuana every day may be functioning at a reduced intellectual level all the time. More recently, the same researchers showed that the ability of a group of long-term heavy marijuana abusers to recall words from a list remained impaired for a week after quitting, but returned to normal within 4 weeks. Thus, some cognitive abilities may be restored in individuals who quit smoking marijuana, even after long-term heavy use.

Workers who smoke marijuana are more likely than their coworkers to have problems on the job. Several studies associate workers' marijuana smoking with increased absences, tardiness, accidents, workers' compensation claims, and job turnover.

A study among postal workers found that employees who tested positive for marijuana on a pre-employment urine drug test had 55 percent more industrial accidents, 85 percent more injuries, and a 75-percent increase in absenteeism compared with those who tested negative for marijuana use.

In another study, heavy marijuana abusers reported that the drug impaired several important measures of life achievement including cognitive abilities, career status, social life, and physical and mental health.

Research has shown that some babies born to women who abused marijuana during their pregnancies display altered responses to visual stimuli, increased tremulousness, and a high-pitched cry, which may indicate neurological problems in development.

During the preschool years, marijuana-exposed children have been observed to perform tasks involving sustained attention and memory more poorly than non-exposed children do. In the school years, these children are more likely to exhibit deficits in problem-solving skills, memory, and the ability to remain attentive. Long-term marijuana abuse can lead to addiction for some people. That is, they abuse the drug compulsively even though it interferes with family, school, work, and recreational activities.

Drug craving and withdrawal symptoms can make it hard for long-term marijuana smokers to stop abusing the drug. People trying to quit report irritability, sleeplessness, and anxiety. They also display increased aggression on psychological tests, peaking approximately one week after the last use of the drug.

Those suffering with an over dependence on marijuana often venture out to abuse other substances, such as alcohol. While addiction to marijuana alone is not seen by all treatment providers as a major concern, most help options would be coupled with treatments for other addictions or diagnoses.

K. J. Gordon

CHAPTER 6

COCAINE

Cocaine is a very powerfully and highly addictive drug that is snorted, sniffed, injected, or smoked. Its street names include coke, snow, flake, blow, and many others.

Cocaine is a stimulant drug that comes in many forms. The powdered, hydrochloride salt form of cocaine can be snorted or dissolved in water and injected.

When cocaine is processed from powder to a free base for smoking, it is called crack. Crack is cocaine that has not been neutralized by an acid to make the hydrochloride salt. This form of cocaine comes in a rock crystal that can be heated and its vapors smoked. The term "crack" refers to the crackling sound heard when it is heated.

Regardless of how cocaine is used or how frequently, a user can experience acute cardiovascular or cerebrovascular emergencies, such as a heart attack or stroke, which could result in sudden death. Cocaine-related deaths are often a result of cardiac arrest or seizure followed by respiratory arrest.

Cocaine is a strong central nervous system stimulant that interferes with the re-absorption process of dopamine. The buildup of dopamine causes continuous stimulation of receiving neurons, which is associated with the euphoria commonly reported by cocaine abusers. Physical effects of cocaine use include constricted blood vessels, dilated pupils, and increased temperature, heart rate, and blood pressure. The duration of cocaine's immediate euphoric effects, which include hyper-stimulation, reduced fatigue, and mental alertness, depends on how it is brought into the body.

The faster the absorption of the drug, the more intense the high, and the shorter the high lasts. The high from snorting cocaine might last 15 to 30 minutes, while that from smoking may last 5 to 10 minutes. Increased use can reduce the period of time a user feels high and increase the risk of addiction. Some users of cocaine report feelings of restlessness, irritability, and anxiety. A tolerance to the "high" may develop—many addicts report that they seek but fail to achieve as much pleasure as they did from their first exposure.

Some users will increase their doses to intensify and prolong the euphoric effects. While tolerance to the high can occur, users can also become more sensitive to cocaine's anesthetic and convulsive effects without increasing the dose taken. This increased sensitivity may explain some deaths occurring after apparently low doses of cocaine. Use of cocaine in a binge, during which the drug is taken repeatedly and at increasingly high doses, may lead to a state of increasing irritability, restlessness, and paranoia. This can result in a period of full-blown paranoid psychosis, in which the user loses touch with reality and experiences auditory hallucinations. Other complications associated with cocaine use include disturbances in heart rhythm and heart attacks, chest pain and respiratory failure, strokes, seizures and headaches, and gastrointestinal complications such as abdominal pain and nausea. Because cocaine has a tendency to decrease appetite, many chronic users can become malnourished.

Different means of taking cocaine can produce different adverse effects. Regularly snorting cocaine, for example, can lead to loss of the sense of smell, nosebleeds, problems with swallowing, hoarseness, and a chronic runny nose.

Ingesting cocaine can cause severe bowel gangrene due to reduced blood flow. People who inject cocaine can experience severe allergic reactions and, as with all injecting drug users, are at increased risk for contracting HIV and other blood-borne diseases.

When people mix cocaine and alcohol, they are compounding the danger each drug poses and are unknowingly forming a complex chemical experiment within their bodies. NIDA-funded researchers have found that the human liver combines cocaine and alcohol and manufactures a third substance, cocaethylene that intensifies cocaine's euphoric effects, while potentially increasing the risk of sudden death.

CHAPTER 7

ALCOHOL

Alcohol is one of the most commonly abused drug in the United States. For most people who drink, alcohol is a pleasant accompaniment to social activities. Moderate alcohol use, up to two drinks per day for men and one drink per day for women and older people, is not harmful for most adults. (A standard drink is one 12-ounce bottle or can of either beer or wine cooler, one 5-ounce glass of wine, or 1.5 ounces of 80-proof distilled spirits.)

Currently, nearly 14 million Americans, 1 in every 13 adults, abuse alcohol or are alcoholics. Several million more adults engage in risky drinking that could lead to alcohol problems. These patterns include binge drinking and heavy drinking on a regular basis. In addition, 53 percent of men and women in the United States report that one or more of their close relatives have a drinking problem.

The consequences of alcohol misuse are serious—in many cases, life threatening. Heavy drinking can increase the risk for certain cancers, especially those of the liver, esophagus, throat, and larynx (voice box). Heavy drinking can also cause liver cirrhosis, immune system problems, brain damage, and harm to the fetus during pregnancy.

In addition, drinking increases the risk of death from automobile crashes as well as recreational and on-the-job injuries. Furthermore, both homicides and suicides are more likely to be committed by someone who has been drinking. In purely economic terms, alcohol-related problems cost society approximately $185 billion per year. In human terms, the costs cannot be calculated.

Alcoholism, also known as "alcohol dependence," is a disease that includes four symptoms:

- **Craving:** A strong need, or compulsion, to drink.

- **Loss of control:** The inability to limit ones drinking on any given occasion.

- **Physical dependence:** Withdrawal symptoms, such as nausea, sweating, shakiness, and anxiety, occur when alcohol use is stopped after a period of heavy drinking.

- **Tolerance:** The need to drink greater amounts of alcohol in order to "get high."

Although some people are able to recover from alcoholism without help, the majority of alcoholics need assistance. With treatment and support, many individuals are able to stop drinking and rebuild their lives.

Many people wonder why some individuals can use alcohol without problems but others cannot. One important reason has to do with genetics. Scientists have found that having an alcoholic family member makes it more likely that if you choose to drink you too may develop alcoholism.

Genes, however, are not the whole story. In fact, scientists now believe that certain factors in a person's environment influence whether a person with a genetic risk for alcoholism ever develops the disease. A person's risk for developing alcoholism can increase based on the person's environment, including where and how he or she lives; family, friends, and culture; peer pressure; and even how easy it is to get alcohol.

Alcohol abuse differs from alcoholism in that it does not include an extremely strong craving for alcohol, loss of control over drinking, or physical dependence. Alcohol abuse is defined as a pattern of drinking that results in one or more of the following situations within a 12-month period:

- Failure to fulfill major work, school, or home responsibilities

- Drinking in situations that are physically dangerous, such as while driving a car or operating machinery

- Having recurring alcohol-related legal problems, such as being arrested for driving under the influence of alcohol or for physically hurting someone while drunk

- Continued drinking despite having ongoing relationship problems that are caused or worsened by the drinking.

Although alcohol abuse is basically different from alcoholism, many effects of alcohol abuse are also experienced by alcoholics. Alcoholism can be treated, but a cure is not yet available. In other words, even if an alcoholic has been sober for a long time and has regained health, he or she remains susceptible to relapse and must continue to avoid all alcoholic beverages. "Cutting down" on drinking doesn't work; cutting out alcohol is necessary for a successful recovery. However, even individuals who are determined to stay sober may suffer one or several "slips," or relapses, before achieving long-term sobriety.

Relapses are very common and do not mean that a person has failed or cannot recover from alcoholism. Keep in mind, too, that every day that a recovering alcoholic has stayed sober prior to a relapse is extremely valuable time, both to the individual and to his or her family. If a relapse occurs, it is very important to try to stop drinking once again and to get whatever additional support you need to abstain from drinking.

CHAPTER 8

PRESCRIPTION DRUGS

OxyContin, Vicodin and other prescription medications are currently the most commonly abused drugs in the United States. They can have effects similar to heroin when taken in doses or in ways other than prescribed by medical professionals. Research now suggests that prescription opiate abuse may be a gateway into heroin abuse.

Nearly half of the young people who inject heroin surveyed in three recent studies done by the National Institute on Drug Abuse reported abusing prescription opioids before starting to use heroin. Some individuals reported taking up heroin because it is cheaper and easier to obtain than prescription opioids. Many of these young people also report that crushing prescription opioid pills to snort or inject the powder provided their initiation into these methods of drug administration.

Prescription drugs are used as pain relievers, tranquilizers, stimulants, and sedatives and are very useful treatment tools, but sometimes people do not take them as instructed by medical professionals. When prescription drugs are abused they are highly addictive and are as harmful as street drugs.

All pain relieving drugs make surgery possible, and enable many individuals with chronic pain to live productive lives. Most people who take prescription medications use them responsibly, as prescribed by their doctor. However, the inappropriate or non-medical use of prescription medications is a serious public health concern. Non-medical or self-prescribed use of prescription medications like opioids, central nervous system (CNS) depressants, and stimulants can lead to addiction, characterized by compulsive drug seeking and use.

Patients, healthcare professionals, and pharmacists all have roles in preventing misuse and addiction to prescription medications. For example, when a doctor prescribes a pain relief medication, CNS depressant, or stimulant, the patient should follow the directions for use carefully, learn what effects the medication could have, and determine any potential interactions with other medications. The patient should also read all information provided by the pharmacist.

Physicians and other healthcare providers should screen for any type of substance abuse during routine history-taking, with questions about which prescriptions and over-the-counter (OTC) medicines the patient is taking and why. Providers should note any rapid increases in the amount of a medication needed or frequent requests for refills before the quantity prescribed should have been used, as these may be indicators of abuse.

While many prescription medications can be abused or misused, these three classes are most commonly abused:

Opioids - often prescribed to treat pain

CNS Depressants – used to treat anxiety as well as sleep disorders

Stimulants - prescribed to treat narcolepsy and attention deficit/hyperactivity disorder

<u>Opioids</u>

Opioids are frequently prescribed by medical doctors to relieve pain. And, when taken exactly as prescribed, opioids can be used to manage pain effectively. Studies have shown that properly managed medical use of opioid analgesic compounds is safe and rarely causes addiction. Among the compounds that fall within this class, sometimes referred to as narcotics, are morphine, codeine, and related medications. Morphine is often used before or after surgery to alleviate severe pain. Codeine is used for milder pain.

Other examples of opioids that can be prescribed to alleviate pain include oxycodone (OxyContin—an oral, controlled release form of the drug); propoxyphene (Darvon); hydrocodone (Vicodin); hydromorphone (Dilaudid); and meperidine (Demerol), which is used less often because of its side effects.

In addition to their effective pain relieving properties, some of these medications can be used to relieve severe diarrhea (Lomotil, for example, which is diphenoxylate) or severe coughs (codeine).

When introduced inside the body, opioids locate the pain receivers in the brain, and change the way the user experiences the pain. In addition, opioid medications can affect regions of the brain that mediate what we perceive as pleasure, resulting in the initial euphoria that many opioids produce. They can also produce drowsiness, cause constipation, and, depending upon the amount taken, depress breathing. Taking a large single dose could cause severe respiratory depression or death.

Opioids are only safe to use with other medications under a physician's supervision. Typically, they should not be used with substances such as alcohol, antihistamines, barbiturates, or benzodiazepines. Since these substances slow breathing, their combined effects could lead to life-threatening respiratory depression. Long-term use also can lead to physical dependence—the body adapts to the presence of the substance and withdrawal symptoms occur if use is reduced abruptly. This can also include tolerance, which means that higher doses of a medication must be taken to obtain the same initial effects.

Note that physical dependence is not the same as addiction—physical dependence can occur even with appropriate long-term use of opioid and other medications. Addiction, as noted earlier, is defined as compulsive, often uncontrollable drug use in spite of negative consequences. Individuals taking prescribed opioid medications should not only be given these medications under appropriate medical supervision, but also should be medically supervised when stopping use in order to reduce or avoid withdrawal symptoms.

Symptoms of withdrawal can include restlessness, muscle and bone pain, insomnia, diarrhea, vomiting, cold flashes with goose bumps ("cold turkey"), and involuntary leg movements.

Individuals who become addicted to prescription medications can be treated. Options for effective treatment are drawn from research on treating heroin addiction. Some pharmacological examples of available treatments include:

• Methadone, a synthetic opioid that blocks the effects of heroin and other opioids, eliminates withdrawal symptoms and relieves cravings. It has been used for over 30 years to treat people addicted to opioids.

• Buprenorphine, another synthetic opioid, is a recent addition to the arsenal of medications for treating addiction to heroin and other opiates.

• Naltrexone is a long-acting opioid blocker often used with highly motivated individuals in treatment programs promoting complete abstinence. Naltrexone also is used to prevent relapse.

• Naloxone counteracts the effects of opioids and is

used to treat overdoses.

Central Nervous System (CNS) Depressants

CNS depressants slow normal brain function. In higher doses, some CNS depressants can become general anesthetics. Tranquilizers and sedatives are examples of CNS depressants. CNS depressants can be divided into two groups, based on their chemistry and pharmacology:

- Barbiturates, such as mephobarbital (Mebaral) and pentobarbital sodium (Nembutal), which are used to treat anxiety, tension, and sleep disorders.

- Benzodiazepines, such as diazepam (Valium), chlordiazepoxide HCl (Librium), and alprazolam (Xanax), which can be prescribed to treat anxiety, acute stress reactions, and panic attacks. Benzodiazepines that have a more sedating effect, such as estazolam (ProSom), can be prescribed for short-term treatment of sleep disorders.

There are many CNS depressants, and most act on the brain similarly—they affect the neurotransmitter gamma-aminobutyric acid (GABA). Neurotransmitters are brain chemicals that facilitate communication between brain cells. GABA works by decreasing brain activity.

Although different classes of CNS depressants work

in unique ways, ultimately it is their ability to increase GABA activity that produces a drowsy or calming effect. Despite these beneficial effects for people suffering from anxiety or sleep disorders, barbiturates and benzodiazepines can be addictive and should be used only as prescribed.

CNS depressants should not be combined with any medication or substance that causes drowsiness, including prescription pain medicines, certain OTC cold and allergy medications, or alcohol. If combined, they can slow breathing, or slow both the heart and respiration, which can be fatal. Discontinuing prolonged use of high doses of CNS depressants can lead to withdrawal. Because they work by slowing the brain's activity, a potential consequence of abuse is that when one stops taking a CNS depressant, the brain's activity can rebound to the point that seizures can occur.

Someone thinking about ending their use of a CNS depressant, or who has stopped and is suffering withdrawal, should speak with a physician and seek medical treatment. In addition to medical supervision, counseling in an in-patient or out-patient setting can help people who are overcoming addiction to CNS depressants. For example, cognitive-behavioral therapy has been used successfully to help individuals in treatment for abuse of benzodiazepines.

This type of therapy focuses on modifying a patient's thinking, expectations, and behaviors while simultaneously increasing their skills for coping with various life stressors. Often the abuse of CNS depressants occurs in conjunction with the abuse of another substance or drug, such as alcohol or cocaine. In these cases of poly-drug abuse, the treatment approach should address the multiple addictions.

Stimulants

Stimulants increase alertness, attention, and energy, which are accompanied by increases in blood pressure, heart rate, and respiration. Historically, stimulants were used to treat asthma and other respiratory problems, obesity, neurological disorders, and a variety of other ailments. As their potential for abuse and addiction became apparent, the use of stimulants began to wane.

Now, stimulants are prescribed for treating only a few health conditions, including narcolepsy, attention-deficit hyperactivity disorder (ADHD), and depression that has not responded to other treatments. Stimulants may also be used for short-term treatment of obesity and for patients with asthma. Stimulants such as dextroamphetamine (Dexedrine) and methylphenidate (Ritalin) have chemical structures that are similar to key brain neurotransmitters called monoamines, which include norepinephrine and dopamine.

Stimulants increase the levels of these chemicals in the brain and body. This, in turn, increases blood pressure and heart rate, constricts blood vessels, increases blood glucose, and opens up the pathways of the respiratory system. In addition, the increase in dopamine is associated with a sense of euphoria that can accompany the use of stimulants. Research indicates that people with ADHD do not become addicted to stimulant medications, such as Ritalin, when taken in the form and dosage prescribed.

However, when misused, stimulants can be addictive. The consequences of stimulant abuse can be extremely dangerous. Taking high doses of a stimulant can result in an irregular heartbeat, dangerously high body temperatures, and/or the potential for cardiovascular failure or seizures. Taking high doses of some stimulants repeatedly over a short period of time can lead to hostility or feelings of paranoia in some individuals. Stimulants should not be mixed with antidepressants or over the counter cold medicines containing decongestants. Antidepressants may enhance the effects of a stimulant, and stimulants in combination with decongestants may cause blood pressure to become dangerously high or lead to irregular heart rhythms.

Treatment of addiction to prescription stimulants, such as methylphenidate and amphetamines, is based on behavioral therapies proven effective for treating cocaine or methamphetamine addiction. At this time, there are no proven medications for the treatment of stimulant addiction. Antidepressants, however, may be used to manage the symptoms of depression that can accompany early abstinence from stimulants.

Depending on the patient's situation, the first step in treating prescription stimulant addiction may be to slowly decrease the drug's dose and attempt to treat withdrawal symptoms. This process of detoxification could then be followed with one of many behavioral therapies.

Contingency management, for example, improves treatment outcomes by enabling patients to earn vouchers for drug-free urine tests; the vouchers can be exchanged for items that promote healthy living. Cognitive-behavioral therapies, which teach patients skills to recognize risky situations, avoid drug use, and cope more effectively with problems, are proving beneficial. Recovery support groups may also be effective in conjunction with a behavioral therapy.

THE FOREVER FIGHT

PART II

ON ADDICTION & RECOVERY

THE FOREVER FIGHT

CHAPTER 9

IDENTIFYING A DRUG PROBLEM

When using mentally altering substances like drugs, you can quickly become addicted without being aware of it. In order to recognize a problem, you first need to evaluate your drug use.

Do you sometimes think you have a drug problem? If the answer is yes, you probably do have an issue with addiction. Drug abusers often deny that they have a problem, or they hide from it by making excuses. It is a natural reaction to defend yourself and your behaviors. But, your defenses break down once in a while, and hint at your inner truth. So, if you sometimes think you have a problem, it is highly probable that you do.

Now think about how you feel the morning after heavily using. Your body aches, your head is cloudy, you feel guilty for over-using and promise yourself you'll stop. You decide that you won't use at all that day. You feel beaten and broken and want to do something about it.

Your defenses are down and you are vulnerable to your own rational thoughts.

As the day goes on, though, your defenses start coming back up again and you begin excusing yourself for the previous day's binge. You start to make excuses for your over-indulgence. You tell yourself you were having a bad day, you didn't eat enough, you were really stressed out, or some other excuse. So, you decide to let yourself use "just a little". After all, you were having a bad day yesterday and today won't be the same. And the cycle continues.

Sound familiar? If so, you are not alone! You may go through this hundreds of times before you recognize that there's a pattern going on. Almost all drug or alcohol abusers go through this cycle.

When you decide to really face the possibility that you have a problem, how do you identify it? The answer is really quite simple. You have a problem when you use too much, too often, and the use is out of control. But you have to be your own judge and be honest with yourself. Pay attention to your feelings.

You may want to write down how you feel about

your drug use. Sometimes seeing the words can help you face the problem and start helping yourself. Let's take a look at a few more questions that can help you identify if you have a drug problem. Answer the following questions honestly.

1. Have you ever felt you should cut down on your drug use or drinking?

2. Do you ever use drugs or drink when you're alone?

3. Have you ever used more of a drug or drank more than you intended in a given period of time?

4. Have you ever used drugs for a longer period of time than you originally intended?

5. Have you ever used more than one drug at a time?

6. Concerning your use of drugs or drinking, has anyone ever told you that you use too much?

7. Have you ever taken one drug to overcome the effects of another?

8. Have you ever thought that your life might be better if you didn't take drugs or drink alcohol?

9. Have you ever felt angry at yourself or guilty because of your drug use or drinking?

10. Do you regularly use a drug or drink at certain times of the day or on certain occasions, for example, when you go to bed, when you wake up, before or after a meal, or before or after sex?

11. Have you ever lied about your drug use or drinking to family members or friends?

12. Have you ever lied to a doctor or faked symptoms to get prescription drugs?

13. Have you ever stolen drugs or alcohol?

14. Have you ever stolen money or material goods that you could sell to obtain drugs or alcohol?

15. Have you ever done things to obtain drugs or alcohol that you later regretted?

16. Has your drug use or drinking ever caused problems for you with school or with work?

17. Have you noticed that you need to use more and more of a drug or drink more to get you high?

18. Do you experience withdrawal symptoms when you go without drugs or drinking for a few days?

19. Do you panic when your drug or alcohol supply gets low?

20. Have you ever done something when you were high or drunk that you felt guilty about later?

21. Have you ever gotten into fights when high on drugs or drunk?

22. Have you ever been arrested for any drug-related activity (including possession or a DUI)?

23. Have you ever been diagnosed with a medical problem related to your drug use or drinking?

24. Have you ever overdosed on a drug?

25. Have you ever attended a treatment program specifically related to drug use or alcoholism?

26. Have you associated with people with whom you normally wouldn't just so you could have access to drugs or alcohol?

27. Have you stopped associating with any of your friends because they don't use drugs or drink as much as you?

If you answered "yes" to any two of these questions, this is a sign that you may have an addiction problem. If you answered "yes" to any three, the chances are that you do have an addiction problem. If you answered "yes" to four or more, you definitely have an addiction problem. But this test is just a tool.

You have become addicted to drugs or alcohol when you start needing to use more to get the same affects, and you start to feel as if you can not go throughout your day without them. You may try to quit, but the withdrawal symptoms are just too much to take so you continue using.

Another good way to identify a drug addiction problem is to write things down. Again, you need to be brutally honest with yourself when you answer the following questions. Take your time and list everything you can think of. The purpose of this exercise is to realize what your addiction has done to your life.

1. **History:** Go back to the start of your alcohol or drug addiction history. List each drug, and alcohol individually and trace the pattern of your life. What age did you start? When did you start increasing either the quantity or frequency of use of each substance? This will show you if you have increased tolerance and if you have become dependent on certain drugs. Something to be noted is that if you

have been only addicted to marijuana, if you decide to quit the marijuana and start alcohol, there is a high probability that you will again become addicted with time.

If you have a family history of alcoholism or drug addiction you may be more susceptible to dependency. Part of this is genetic and also a learned model.

2. **Health:** Look at your physical health. List effects or any accidents, which may have been due to alcohol or drug use.

3. **Concerned Persons:** Think of comments others have made and the effect you have made on them because of your alcohol or drug addiction. Did you miss birthdays? Did you break promises? List each person personally and all consequences you remember.

4. **Irrational, or Dangerous Behavior:** List times you took careless actions that put yourself or others in danger. List things you would not do if not using alcohol or drugs.

5. **Sex:** Look at your sex life. Did your addiction to

drugs or alcohol allow you to have sex without knowing someone? Did you take health risks such as lack of birth control or unprotected sex? Did the use of alcohol or drugs put you in danger of STD's and Aids?

6. **Work:** List examples of days missed, being late, quitting or being fired from work. Did you get demoted, laid off or miss promotions or pay raises due to drug or alcohol use?

7. **Social Life and Friends:** How have your social activities and friends changed while using alcohol or drugs. Did you lose or drift away from non-drinkers or drug users? Did you become a part of a drug culture? Did you miss your partner's or children's activities when they wanted you to participate?

8. **Money:** Write down all legal costs, treatment expenses, loss of work pay, and how much you spent weekly on your alcohol or drug addiction. Add the years up to determine the loss. You may find you could own a house or have a large savings with the money spent on alcohol and drugs.

9. **Preoccupation:** Did you start looking forward to or leaving work early to get alcohol or drugs? Did you use alcohol or drugs on the way to, or during work? Did you hide your drugs so nobody could use or throw them away?

10. **Control:** Did you make promises to cut down on either drugs or alcohol that you were not able to keep? Did you quit after a DUI and then begin again?

11. **Emotions and Feelings:** What did alcohol and drug use do to your feelings? List the way they affected fear, anger, love, guilt, depression, loneliness and hurt. What is the difference between when you are using alcohol or drugs and when you are sober?

12. **Spiritual and Character:** How are you different from what you desired or planned your life to be at this age? Are you divorced, giving up on God or your religious believes and full of selfishness for only the addiction and you? What are your spiritual beliefs? Write them down, and if you are able, ask your God to help remove your alcohol or drug addiction for things that build you and others up.

After completion of the exercise, do you think you have a problem? If so , decide to start your recovery plan by writing a Dear John letter to the alcohol or drug addiction itself. List what these substances did for your life including the damage, and why you need to say good bye.

In the next chapter we will review ways to recognize if a loved one you suspect is, in fact, struggling with a drug problem.

THE FOREVER FIGHT

CHAPTER 10

SIGNS OF ADDICTION IN OTHERS

You can recognize signs of drug abuse in those around you by paying close attention to their behavior. Review the questions from chapter 9 once again and see if you can identify any of the symptoms of a drug problem in them. Alienation from others, severe changes in behavior, increased defensives are all signs that a user has a problem.

Drug addicts will give up previously enjoyable activities that they would participate in. Their lives will become consumed with getting drugs and using drugs. Their physical appearance will change drastically. They will start missing work or school and the quality of their work will suffer.

To identify what type of drug your loved one might be using, compare the changes you have noticed in them to the following list of common signs of specific drug use.

Marijuana

• Rapid, loud talking and bursts of laughter, followed by sleepiness

•Forgetfulness in conversation

• Inflammation in whites of eyes; pupils unlikely to be dilated

• Odor similar to burnt rope on clothing or breath

• Tendency to drive slowly, below speed limit

• Distorted sense of time, with tendency to overestimate time intervals

• Use or possession of paraphernalia including roach clip, packs of rolling papers, pipes or bongs

Stimulants

(Cocaine, Amphetamines, Methamphetamines)

• Dilated pupils (when large amounts are taken)

- Dry mouth and nose, bad breath, frequent lip licking

- Excessive activity, difficulty sitting still, lack of interest in food or sleep

- Irritable, argumentative, nervous

- Talkative, but conversation often lacks continuity; and changes subjects rapidly

- Runny nose, cold or chronic sinus/nasal problems, nose bleeds

- Use or possession of paraphernalia including small spoons, razor blades, mirror, little bottles of white powder and plastic, glass or metal straws

Depressants

(Barbiturates, Benzodiazepine)

- Similar symptoms as alcohol intoxication, without the smell of alcohol on the breath (depressants are frequently used with alcohol)

- Lack of facial expression or animation

- Flat affect

- Flaccid appearance

- Slurred speech

Narcotics

(Heroin, Codeine, Morphine, Vicodin)

- Lethargy, drowsiness

- Constricted pupils fail to respond to light

- Redness and raw nostrils from inhaling heroin in power form

- Scars (tracks) on inner arms or other parts of body, from needle injections

- Use or possession of paraphernalia, including syringes, bent spoons, bottle caps, eye droppers, rubber tubing, cotton and needles

- Slurred speech

Hallucinogens

(LSD, mescaline)

- Extremely dilated pupils

- Warm skin, excessive perspiration and body odor

- Distorted sense of sight, hearing, touch; distorted image of self and time perception

- Mood and behavior changes, the extent depending on emotional state of the user and environmental conditions

- Unpredictable flashback episodes even long after withdrawal (although these are rare)

Dissociative Anesthetics

(PCP)

- Unpredictable behavior; mood may swing from passiveness to violence for no apparent reason

- Symptoms of intoxication

- Disorientation; agitation and violence if exposed to excessive sensory stimulation

- Fear, terror

- Rigid muscles

- Strange gait

- Deadened sensory perception (may experience severe injuries while appearing not to notice)

- Pupils may appear dilated

- Mask like facial appearance

- Floating pupils, appear to follow a moving object

- Comatose (unresponsive) if large amount consumed; eyes may be open or closed

Inhalants

(Glue, Vapor producing solvents, Propellants)

- Substance odor on breath and clothes

THE FOREVER FIGHT

- Runny nose

- Watering eyes

- Drowsiness or unconsciousness

- Poor muscle control

- Prefers group activity to being alone

- Presence of bags or rags containing dry plastic cement or other solvent at home, in locker at school or at work

- Discarded whipped cream, spray paint or similar chargers (users of nitrous oxide)
- Small bottles labeled "incense" (users of butyl nitrite)

CHAPTER 11

HOW ADDICTION WORKS

Medical research shows two major causes of physical addiction. First, your cells adapt to the drug and, second, your metabolism becomes more efficient.

To your cells, the drugs you're using become a way of life. Every time you use a drug, your blood carries it to every cell in your body, and your cells adjust. They grow to expect these doses on schedule. Your body on drugs is your new normal - and being off the drugs becomes the abnormality.

Your cells learn to cope with various drugs by defending themselves against the drugs' toxic effects. Cell walls harden to retain stability and reduce toxic damage.

But as your cells get tougher to fight against drugs, gradually more and more can be consumed. Your tolerance increases.

In the long run, however, cell walls break down. At this point, your cells not only lose their ability to keep toxins out but also become unable to retain essential nutrients. Many of them stop functioning altogether or start functioning abnormally. That's when your organs (heart, brain, liver, or lungs), which are nothing more than whole systems of cells, begin to fail.

The problem with metabolism is that it is intimately connected to diet. Your body metabolizes food (breaks it down into its constituent parts) to get vital nutrients to all the cells. To serve this purpose, your body can metabolize many different foods and can learn how to gain nutrients from almost any kind of food you give it.

Metabolism also helps to rid the body of unwanted toxins. The liver is the key organ in this process. The liver "sees" drugs and alcohol as unwanted toxins and begins producing enzymes that will help eliminate them from the body. It produces a different combination of enzymes for each drug. The liver also becomes extremely efficient at producing these enzymes. The more it "sees" a particular drug, the more efficiently it produces the enzymes that inactivate, or fight that drug and its effects on the body.

Thus, a drug that you use often will get eliminated from the body with greater and greater efficiency. It's as if the liver begins to "expect" that drug and has enzymes ready and waiting. This is a key reason that tolerance increases, and why it takes greater and greater doses of a drug to get the same original effects.

Yet your personal metabolism works differently from anyone else's. Studies show that each individual has a unique biochemical makeup and that individuals differ greatly from one another in the way they metabolize different foods, drugs and toxins.

Also, the mixture of bio-chemicals varies for each kind of food you ingest. For example, your body uses different bio-chemicals to metabolize the different food types. Meats, grains, vegetables, beans, fruits, and nuts are all processed differently. Similarly, you need a whole different biochemical preparedness to handle drugs, alcohol, sugars, chemical additives, and toxins. Because your body adjusts to whatever diet you give it, the most frequent foods in your diet come to be expected by it. Biochemical pathways become established the more they are used. So, if your body doesn't get an expected food or drug, you actually begin to crave it.

In fact, your body becomes addicted to the foods you give it the most. Your metabolism so completely adjusts to your regular diet that any change from this diet becomes increasingly difficult. Ask anyone who has attempted a major shift in diet. For example, if you eat meat regularly, your metabolism will take a long time to adjust to a vegetarian diet. Although the same nutrients are available, your body doesn't have the biochemical preparedness. The ability is there. Your body can metabolize vegetarian meals. No problem. But to gain the same efficiency with a new diet can take from one to seven years.

The important thing to remember is that Metabolism depends on diet. For our purposes, "diet" includes not only the nutritious foods but also the non-nutritious foods, such as sugar and alcohol, as well as other substances, such as chemical additives in foods, environmental toxins, and drugs.

You can change your metabolism if you change your diet. Although it will take a long time to change your metabolism significantly, you'll feel incredible improvements after just a few months.

We become addicted to drugs partly as a way to avoid life's misery. In our minds at least, we become unwilling to suffer.

Real life is loaded with suffering. We not only experience countless physical pains but also must cope with psychological pain. Many events make us ache inside.

Things happen that cause us to feel sad, miserable, angry, nervous, tense, disgusted, confused, weakened, tortured, cheated, abused, frightened, or upset.

But we can avoid these feelings, at least for the moment, by using drugs. We can do drugs and almost instantly feel "high." We can forget about life for a while. We can experience pleasure, excitement, power, courage, thrills, joy, enchantment, and a sense of connection with other people and the world around us.

Of course, in the long run drugs become less and less effective at bringing these benefits. Over time, the drugs themselves start causing suffering. Soon, we find that we are using drugs to relieve the misery that drugs themselves have caused. This is known as the "vicious cycle of addiction."

Life doesn't feel too good. Try this drug or that drug, and things feel better. Come down off the drug, and things feel worse, just a little worse than they did before you took the drug in the first place. No matter what, you will need to use the drug to feel good again. Gradually, your biochemistry changes. Your brain learns that it doesn't have to keep producing the chemicals that make you feel good. These chemicals keep appearing without the brain having to do any work. That's why each time you try to get off the drugs, you feel a little worse than the time before. It becomes harder and harder for you to get off the drugs because you feel so bad whenever you try to stop.

And it all started with suffering, with your inability to accept suffering as an intimate part of life. You can break a drug habit anywhere along the way, or never start with drugs at all, simply by accepting life's suffering and facing the suffering head-on.

This doesn't mean that you will live a sad, miserable, and tormented life. There are plenty of ways you can face your suffering and then cope with it. In fact, once you learn these ways and begin using some of them, you'll feel as if your spirit has been renewed.

Of course, it's your choice. If you choose drugs to cope with life's suffering, you choose a buy-now-pay-later method. It works in the moment, but it just postpones the suffering. And by postponing it, it builds up, so that when you finally do face it, the suffering is immense.

Addiction Recovery is not easy; it's a lifelong journey which we will cover in the next chapter. The detoxification from drugs might take a week or two, but the long-term withdrawal, the period of time when your biochemistry (and thus your physical and mental health) returns to normal, can take years. Luckily, during recovery, you gradually feel a little bit better, day by day.

THE FOREVER FIGHT

CHAPTER 12

ADDICTION RECOVERY

Addiction is a chronic disease that cannot be cured after a few days of not using drugs or alcohol. Most patients need long-term or repeated care to stop using completely and recover their lives. According to SAMHSA's National Survey on Drug Use and Health in 2014, only 4.2 million or 18.5 percent of those who needed treatment received any substance use treatment that year. Of these, about 2.6 million people received treatment at specialty treatment centers.

Addiction treatment must help the person stop using drugs, stay drug-free, and be productive in the family, at work, and in society. Scientific research conducted since the mid-1970s, has found that any effective treatment program should follow and understand the following principles:

- That Addiction is a complex, but treatable disease that affects brain function and behavior.

- No single treatment is right for everyone.

- People need to have quick access to treatment.

- Effective treatment addresses all of the patient's needs, not just his or her drug use.

- Staying in treatment long enough is critical.

- Counseling and other behavioral therapies are the most commonly used forms of treatment.

- Medications are often an important part of treatment, especially when combined with behavioral therapies.

- Treatment plans must be reviewed often and modified to fit the patient's changing needs.

- Treatment should address other possible mental disorders.

- Medically assisted detoxification is only the first stage of treatment.

- Treatment does not need to be voluntary to be effective.

- Drug use during treatment must be monitored continuously.

- Treatment programs should test patients for HIV/AIDS, hepatitis B and C, tuberculosis, and other infectious diseases as well as teach them about steps they can take to reduce their risk of these illnesses.

Successful treatment has several steps, which we will review in the upcoming chapters. These include:

- Detoxification (the process by which the body rids itself of a drug)

- Behavioral counseling

- Medication (for opioid, tobacco, or alcohol addiction)

- Evaluation and treatment for co-occurring mental health issues such as depression and anxiety

- Long-term follow-up to prevent relapse

A range of care with a tailored treatment program and follow-up options can be crucial to success. Treatment should include both medical and mental health services as needed. Follow-up care may include community or family-based recovery support systems. Medications can be used to manage withdrawal symptoms, prevent relapse, and treat co-occurring conditions.

Medications help suppress withdrawal symptoms during detoxification, the first step in treatment. Patients who do not receive any further treatment after detoxification usually resume their drug use. One study of treatment facilities found that medications were used in almost 80 percent of detoxifications (SAMHSA, 2014). Patients can also use medications to help re-establish normal brain function and decrease cravings during treatment of opioid (heroin, prescription pain relievers), tobacco (nicotine), and alcohol addiction. Scientists currently are developing other medications to treat stimulant (cocaine, methamphetamine) and cannabis (marijuana) addiction.

People who use more than one drug, which is very common, need treatment for all of the substances they use. Methadone (Dolophine®, Methadose®), buprenorphine (Suboxone®, Subutex®), and naltrexone (Vivitrol®) are used to treat opioid addiction. Acting on the same targets in the brain as heroin and morphine, methadone and buprenorphine suppress withdrawal symptoms and relieve cravings. Naltrexone blocks the effects of opioids at their receptor sites in the brain and should be used only in patients who have already been detoxified. These medications are prescribed to help patients reduce drug seeking and related criminal behavior, and help them become more open to behavioral treatments.

Three medications have been FDA-approved for treating alcohol addiction and a fourth, topiramate, has shown promise in clinical trials (large-scale studies with people). The first, Naltrexone, blocks opioid receptors that are involved in the rewarding effects of drinking and in the craving for alcohol. It reduces relapse to heavy drinking and is highly effective in some patients. Genetic differences may affect how well the drug works in certain patients.

The second, Acamprosate (Campral®), may reduce symptoms of long-lasting withdrawal, such as insomnia, anxiety, restlessness, and dysphoria (generally feeling unwell or unhappy). It may be more effective in patients with severe addiction. Disulfiram (Antabuse®) is the third, which interferes with the breakdown of alcohol and is for people who are highly motivated to quit drinking. Acetaldehyde builds up in the body, leading to unpleasant reactions that include flushing (warmth and redness in the face), nausea, and irregular heartbeat if the patient drinks alcohol. Other medications are available to treat possible mental health conditions, such as depression or anxiety that may be contributing to the person's addiction.

Behavioral therapies are also used to treat drug addiction and help patients modify their attitudes and behaviors related to drug use, and increase healthy life skills. Medication, just as detoxing, is only one step on the journey towards recovery. Further treatment is available in different settings with various approaches.

Outpatient behavioral treatment includes a wide variety of programs for patients including routine visits with a behavioral health counselor. Most of the programs involve individual or group drug counseling, or both. These programs typically offer forms of behavioral therapy such as:

- *cognitive-behavioral therapy*, which helps patients recognize, avoid, and cope with the situations in which they are most likely to use drugs, or that will trigger them to use

- *multidimensional family therapy*—developed for adolescents with drug abuse problems as well as their families—which addresses a range of influences on their drug abuse patterns and is designed to improve overall family functioning

- *motivational interviewing,* which makes the most of people's readiness to change their behavior and enter treatment

- *motivational incentives* (contingency management), which uses positive reinforcement to encourage abstinence from drugs

Treatment is sometimes intensive at first, where patients attend multiple outpatient sessions each week. After completing intensive treatment, patients transition to regular outpatient treatment, which meets less often and for fewer hours per week to help sustain their recovery.

In patient rehab programs are typically 1 - 6 month stays at a secluded recovery center. During your stay you will address your problems specifically; the reason why you began using drugs, why you became addicted, and learn new ways to cope with stressors besides using drugs. Inpatient or residential treatment can be very effective, especially for those with co-occurring disorders such as depression. Licensed residential treatment facilities offer 24-hour structured and intensive care, including safe housing and medical attention. Residential treatment facilities may use a variety of therapeutic approaches, and they are generally aimed at helping the patient live a drug-free, crime-free lifestyle after treatment. Examples of residential treatment settings include:

- *Therapeutic communities*, which are highly structured programs in which patients remain at a residence, typically for 6 to 12 months. The entire community, including treatment staff and those in recovery, act as key agents of change, influencing the patient's attitudes, understanding, and behaviors associated with drug use.

- *Shorter-term residential treatment*, which typically focuses on detoxification as well as providing initial intensive counseling and preparation for treatment in a community-based setting.

- *Recovery housing*, which provides supervised, short-term housing for patients, often following other types of inpatient or residential treatment. Recovery housing can help people make the transition to an independent life—for example, helping them learn how to manage finances or seek employment, as well as connecting them to support services in the community.

Scientific research since the mid-1970s shows that drug abuse treatment can help many drug-using criminal offenders change their attitudes, beliefs, and behaviors towards drug abuse; avoid relapse; and successfully remove themselves from a life of substance abuse and crime. Many of the principles of treating drug addiction are similar for people within the criminal justice system as for those in the general population. However, many offenders do not have access to the types of services they need. Treatment that is of poor quality or is not well suited to the needs of offenders may not be effective at reducing drug use and criminal behavior.

In addition to the general principles of treatment, some considerations specific to offenders include the following:

- Treatment should include development of specific cognitive skills to help the offender adjust attitudes and beliefs that lead to drug abuse and crime, such as feeling entitled to have things one's own way or not understanding the consequences of one's behavior. This includes skills related to thinking, understanding, learning, and remembering.

- Treatment planning should include tailored services within the correctional facility as well as transition to community-based treatment after release.

- Ongoing coordination between treatment providers and courts or parole and probation officers is important in addressing the complex needs of offenders re-entering society.

Many rehab facilities are like resorts. They are located in peaceful places with lush, green lawns and plenty of room to move around. This allows individuals to concentrate on becoming healthy in slower pace, stress-free living. Some centers provide activities like boating, fishing, and sports for their patients. By offering these types of activities at the center, patients can find the comfort and support they need to improve and change their lives by staying fit and active. You need to find a place you are comfortable with that has credentials that can be verified. You'll want to be at a place where you can heal, in an environment that is peaceful and professional.

At Rehab you will be part of a community of individuals all trying to get help for their addictions. Many rehab centers operate as a small community with decisions about life at the center made collaboratively. You may be required to take classes or attend lectures about various aspects of drug addiction. These are important because they can help you lay a foundation for life after you are released from the program.

You will also probably have group therapy which will entail talking to others and listening to what they have to say. These sessions will help you get support from other people who are struggling with addiction. When you have other people who are going through the same things that you are, it will help you build a stable mind knowing that you have support all around.

Individual counseling is also part of a drug rehab program. Through individual counseling, you will be able to identify your triggers and the specific reasons why you began using and abusing drugs in the first place. You will be given ways to cope with stressors of life and techniques that you can use to help you stay away from these substances once your rehab program has finished.

Exercise and healthy eating programs will also be a big part of your recovery program. When you eat better and are active, you are better able to heal and concentrate on being clean and sober.

Rehab facilities will teach you about meditation, yoga, eating healthy, and so much more. They can be scary and overwhelming, but they will be intense. You may find yourself angry or resistant, but when you are in a rehab facility, realize that you are there because your drug use got out of control and was damaging your life.

The people in these centers are very supportive and will do everything they can to help you through the process of becoming drug-free. Whether you are there voluntarily or have been ordered into the center for whatever reason, you need to facilitate your healing and make it as easy as possible on yourself. Expect to eat healthier, meet new people, and talk about your problems. You may find it very liberating and when you let the program work for you instead of working against the program, you will be well on your way to a drug free lifestyle.

Most treatments are based on the Minnesota Model, a method of drug addiction treatment focused on a 12-step model recovery. The elements of the Minnesota Model typically include:

- Thorough assessment of all aspects of a the participants physical, emotional, mental, behavioral

- A personalized treatment plan for each participant

- Attendance of 12-step meetings and application of the 12-step philosophy

- Self-reflection with an emphasis on greater acceptance of personal responsibility, changing negative beliefs about one's self and others, and learning new coping skills

- Group and individual therapy (80-90% done in groups)

- Family support, education, and involvement

- Extensive outpatient follow up and support

The Minnesota Model is conducted by a multidisciplinary team of professionals - chemical dependency counselors, psychologists, psychiatrists, nurses, etc. The purpose of this model is to enable addicted individuals to achieve a significant transformation in their basic thinking, feeling and acting in relation to themselves and others. The resulting life change is identified as basically spiritual, though non-religious, in nature and is associated with the positive influence of group affiliation.

The twelve-step program that will be introduced to you at rehab, if you're not already familiar with it, has proven to be quite effective. The steps, when followed, lead to a type of inner peace that will help you stay strong against your addictions when you go back home, and not fall into the same rut that led you there.

During your recovery process, the first step is to rid the drugs from your body. This is called detoxification and it can be very serious if not handled in the correct way.

With detoxification, all traces of the drugs that the body has become dependent on, are removed from your body. This is a scary and sometimes dangerous process. You should not try to detox without the help of a doctor. There are also some drugs that can aid in detox that you might be given, under a doctor's supervision. We will go more in-depth about safe detoxing in the next chapter.

CHAPTER 13

SAFE DETOXING

Drug and alcohol detox is the first and most important step towards addiction recovery. When the body is addicted to any external substance, a chemical change occurs. Detoxing is denying chemicals from your body that it has become used to, and has grown to crave and rely on. When these chemicals are taken away from the body all at once without proper care, a detox can turn from a positive process to a fatal one. Detoxing should be seen as a medical procedure and be handled under the supervision of trained medical professionals.

If you elect to enter an inpatient rehab facility, you will have the guidance and help you need to get through the detox procedure. However, if you decide outpatient or another treatment option is best, you must contact a doctor and be under his or her supervision while you are ridding your body of drugs.

The physical symptoms of detoxification vary according to what type of drugs you are coming off of.

Detoxing will cause the chemical reactions that occur in the body when on the drugs to change. Symptoms range from cold sweats to shaking, to things as serious as convulsions and heart palpitations. Here is what you can expect when detoxing from specific drugs:

<u>Stimulants – (Cocaine, amphetamines)</u>

These drugs enhance nerve cell signaling, depleting the natural signaling abilities of these cells off drugs. This and sleep disturbance are the reasons for the "come down" from cocaine and speed.

<u>Benzodiazepines– (Valium, Xanax, Ativan, Ambien)</u>

Drugs in this category turn down the signal of nerve cells and make you sleepy and relaxed. When these drugs are stopped, the nerves are sensitive to even the smallest stimulation. Taking these drugs out of your system will make you very jittery and shaky. You may have trouble sleeping, and in severe cases, you could have convulsions.

Alcohol – (Beer, Wine, Liquor, Spirits)

Alcohol is a very sneaky drug. With your first drink you feel energized and focused, but after a few drinks, the sedative effects kick in and make you relaxed and clumsy. This occurs because the brain changes and learns how to cope with the sedative effects brought on by the alcohol. Abruptly stopping alcohol, without allowing your brain to readjust, can cause seizures or even heart attack. Hallucinations, sleep disturbance, and anxiety can occur as well.

Opiates – (Heroin, Vicodin)

These drugs are used as pain killers and are meant to soothe and calm the body. Withdrawal from opiates can be particularly painful and severe. Expect sweating, severe muscle aches, nausea, and intense cravings. Because these symptoms are so painful, detoxing from opiates often lead addicts to begin using again.

There are specific drugs that can help with detoxification symptoms. Because some of the symptoms are so severe, having these drugs available can be very important. As with other detoxing techniques, they should be used under the care of a doctor who will monitor your usage throughout the process.

One very effective treatment of opiate withdrawal symptoms is methadone maintenance therapy. It is safe only when administered under the care of a doctor. Taken orally once a day, methadone suppresses narcotic withdrawal for 24 to 36 hours. Because methadone is effective in eliminating withdrawal symptoms, it is used in detoxifying opiate addicts. It is, however, only effective in cases of addiction to heroin, morphine, and other opioid drugs, and it is not an effective treatment for other drugs of abuse.

Methadone reduces the cravings associated with heroin use and blocks the high from heroin, but it does not provide the euphoric rush. Consequently, methadone patients do not experience the extreme highs and lows that result from the waxing and waning of heroin in blood levels. Ultimately, the patient remains physically dependent on the opioid, but is freed from the uncontrolled, compulsive, and disruptive behavior seen in heroin addicts.

Withdrawal from methadone is much slower than that from heroin. As a result, it is possible to maintain an addict on methadone without harsh side effects. Many methadone patients require continuous treatment, sometimes over a period of years.

Physicians prescribe methadone to relieve withdrawal symptoms, reduce the opiate craving, and bring about a biochemical balance in the body. Important elements in heroin treatment include comprehensive social and rehabilitation services.

When methadone is taken under medical supervision, long-term maintenance causes no adverse effects to the heart, lungs, liver, kidneys, bones, blood, brain, or other vital body organs. Methadone produces no serious side effects, although some patients experience minor symptoms such as constipation, water retention, drowsiness, skin rash, excessive sweating, and changes in libido. Once methadone dosage is adjusted and stabilized or tolerance increases, these symptoms usually subside.

Methadone does not impair cognitive functions. It has no adverse effects on mental capability, intelligence, or employability. It is not sedating or intoxicating, nor does it interfere with ordinary activities such as driving a car or operating machinery. Patients are able to feel pain and experience emotional reactions. Most importantly, methadone relieves the craving associated with opiate addiction. For methadone patients, typical street doses of heroin are ineffective at producing euphoria, making the use of heroin less desirable.

Another huge part of safe detoxification has to do with nutrition. Because the body will be going through some harsh abuse, it's important that your body is at its strongest. That means eating healthy and getting some form of exercise. You may want to consult with a nutritionist to be sure that you are getting the proper nutrition, or make your own changes in what you eat so your body is at its peak level of performance.

You will also want to seek psychological help with a counselor or therapist to treat your mental state along with your body. The therapist can help you remain focused on your recovery and take away some of the mindsets that can hinder your recovery.

As mentioned previously, twelve step programs have proven to be very effective in overcoming problems with addiction. These can be great self-help options.

K. J. Gordon

CHAPTER 14

WORKING THE 12 STEPS

All 12 step programs follow similar patterns. Members of a group meet regularly to discuss their experiences, strengths, weaknesses, and hopes. It is understood by all members that everyone is suffering from an illness known as addiction, rather than just a bad habit or poor lifestyle. The key to these programs is getting individuals to take responsibility for their own recovery by relying on a "higher power". Each group member must admit that they have a problem, and open each meeting by addressing to the group with their name and the admission of their problem.

Attendees then share their experiences, challenges, successes, and failures. They also provide peer support for each other. Many people who have joined these groups say they found success that they were unable to find before.

The 12 steps, as outlined by Alcoholics Anonymous,

are:

1. We have admitted we were powerless over alcohol (or drugs) and that our lives had become unmanageable.

2. We have come to believe that a power greater than ourselves could restore us to sanity.

3. We have made a decision to turn our will and our lives over to the care of 'God as we understand him to be'

4. We made a fearless moral inventory of our lives and ourselves. (Have identified any areas of past regret, embarrassment, guilt or anger.

5. We admit to God, to ourselves, and to another human being the exact nature of our wrongs.

6. We are entirely ready to have God remove all these defects of character. (Ready to have a higher power remove the wrongs listed in Step 4)

7. We humbly ask Him to remove our shortcomings.

8. We make a list of all persons we have harmed and are willing to make amends to all of them.

9. We make direct amends to such people wherever possible, except when to do so would injure them or others.

10. We continue to take personal inventory and when we are wrong, we promptly admit it.

11. Through prayer and meditation, we seek to

improve our conscious contact with God, as we understand Him, praying only for knowledge of His will for us and the power to carry that out.

12. Having had a spiritual awakening as the result of these steps, we carry this message to other addicts and practice these principles in all our affairs.

Members of a 12 step program also make several promises to themselves and to others. These promises are:

• If we are painstaking about this phase of our development, we will be amazed before we are halfway through.

• We are going to know a new freedom and a new happiness.

• We will not regret the past nor wish to shut the door on it.

• We will comprehend the word "serenity" and we will know peace.

• No matter how far down the scale we have gone, we will see how our experiences can benefit others.

• The feeling of uselessness and self-pity will disappear.

• We will lose interest in selfish things and gain interest in our fellow man.

• Self-seeking will slip away.

- Our whole attitude and outlook on life will change.
- Fear of people and economic insecurity will leave us.

- We will intuitively know how to handle situations that used to challenge us.

- We will suddenly realize that God is doing for us what we could not do for ourselves.

Opponents of 12 step programs believe that the use of "Higher Power" and God in the steps and mottos is pushing religion on people and is morally wrong if that person doesn't believe in God in the same way as others do. However, you should know that AA and other similar groups are not religious groups. That is why the verbiage "Higher Power" is used along with the phrase "God, as we understand Him to be". The purpose of a 12 step program is to simply deliver addicts from their destructive behaviors and help them become clean and sober. It is a spiritual program in nature, not a religious program. The spiritual aspect helps to advance some people that are incapable of eliminating character defects on their own.

Many people are apprehensive about appearing in front of strangers and sharing their most intimate, personal information. Please remember that 12 step programs are anonymous, and only your first name is shared. If you live in a small town, you may worry that people will recognize you, but keep in mind that those other people are there for the same reason you are and they want to remain anonymous just like you. You may be surprised at the camaraderie you will find when you are with people who share the same experiences that you do.

One of the possible reasons you became addicted to drugs is due to low self-esteem. You need to address self-esteem issues early on in your recovery.

K. J. Gordon

CHAPTER 15

BUILDING YOUR SELF-ESTEEM

It is nearly impossible to effectively journey down the path to recovery without realizing that you deserve to be drug-free. Building your self-esteem requires effort on your part, and, just like during your self-assessment, it also requires personal honesty. Building self-esteem helps not only with personal acceptance, but with staying strong during your recovery as well. To begin with, you need to answer a few questions:

- Do I deserve happiness in my life?

- Should I expect to be accepted by others?

- What do I want out of life?

When you answer these questions honestly, you can begin to acknowledge your strengths and weaknesses. Accepting that you have certain strengths and weaknesses can help you concentrate on the parts of you that need to be worked on and what can help you through.

Remember, you are a unique individual and are no less worthy than anyone else in what you deserve from life. If you hesitated to answer, or answered negatively to any of the questions above, please keep reading. You create your own tomorrow today. Changing a thought process or your inner expectations is essential to recovery.

Positive affirmations are very important in building your self-esteem. They will become your mantra as you work on the parts of you that you want to change. They can also be helpful when you are feeling weak during the recovery process.

A positive affirmation can be anything you want it to be, but it must be positive! Here are a few to consider:

- I deserve to be happy.

- I am a person worthy of respect and acceptance from those around me.

- It's OK to accept a compliment

- I believe that my life has meaning.

- I am a wonderful person who deserves to be sober.

- When I become more confident, I can do anything.

- I am strong and can make it through today.

- I am more than a body; I am a soul and a heart and a spirit and those are parts of me that have to heal so I can be healthy.

Look in the mirror, look into your own eyes, and recite your affirmations over and over again. Change your mindset from not believing what you say to wholeheartedly accepting that it is the truth. Do this several times a day if you have to. Eventually, you'll start believing what you say without having to quiet down those negative thoughts when they creep in.

A part of having low self-esteem involves self-pity. Feeling sorry for yourself when things get rough is a common factor among people with low self-esteem and especially among addicts. Many people listen to their negative inner voices because it's become a way of life.

Self-pity robs you of the joys of life and makes you helpless against your inner demons.

When bad things happen to you, try to focus on the positive things that can come of it. Make time for yourself to recite your positive affirmations. Work hard on focusing on the positives of life. When you're overwhelmed, think, "I'm still alive and I need to be thankful for that."

You may want to try mind mapping. This is a technique used by teachers all over the world and it can do wonders for you when keeping in mind your ultimate goals. Take a piece of paper and make a circle in the center. Inside that circle, write one of your goals. Then take a line and draw it out from the circle. On that line, write a way you can go about achieving that goal. You may want to list things to avoid by starting with "Don't" or "Not".

Once you have your mind map done, carry it with you or post it someplace where you will see it every day. When you have the map to refer to, you will be focusing on your goals and getting away from whatever will hold you back from seeing those goals realized.

Another step towards build1ing self-esteem is to realize that you, as a person, have certain rights. These rights extend to more than just those guaranteed in the constitution. We're talking about moral and ethical rights that you are entitled to. These include the right to:

- Make your own decisions

- Please yourself before you try to please others

- Dignity and respect

- Say "No" if you don't want to do something

- Live without abuse and control from others

- Make mistakes and then learn from them

- Be treated like you treat others, which should be respectfully

The foundation for building self-esteem to engage in codependency and addiction recovery, is built by returning to the child of innocence within. Study and do your own work to become whole, remember this is for your healing. Each person is different and becoming whole will depend on what an individual's experiences have been. The only person in your life at all times, and the only one who knows the truth from your perspective, is you. Stand for the truth in you.

Having the support of your family is also crucial during your recovery period. If you are a family member who has a loved one with an addiction, this is an especially important chapter for you.

CHAPTER 16

INVOLVING THE FAMILY

Admitting a drug or alcohol dependence or addiction to your family is a crucial step towards recovery. If you have been struggling for a long time, your family members probably already know. If not, sit them down and be open and honest with them. Tell them you want their support as you make the necessary steps towards being drug-free. If they don't, just accept it and realize you will need to focus on your recovery with others who will support you.

You should ask those who care about you to be available if you need to talk, but also tell them that it is not their responsibility to cover up your mistakes, relapses, or problems. At all times, you need to respect them and show them that you appreciate their support.

As difficult as it might be for you, it's doubly as difficult for them to watch you going through the pain that you are.

As a family member, of someone who is struggling, you need to be supportive without being an enabler. Here are some things you can do to support your addict.

- Remind them to attend any meetings they need to (AA, NA, etc.)
- Do not loan them money
- Participate in group therapy if asked
- Encourage them to eat healthy and exercise
- Point out when they are engaging in damaging behavior
- Be open to listen when he or she wants to talk
- Do not try to solve all of their problems

You may have to change the way you celebrate family events. This is especially true with people who are trying to overcome alcohol addiction. Often, when some families get together, alcohol is a big part of the celebration. Be understanding if your family member with a problem doesn't want to attend a function. Try to keep alcohol in a separate place where they can't get to it. DO NOT, under any circumstances poke fun at them or try to get them to join in. They are having a hard enough time as it is – they don't need "peer" pressure on top of it all.

Generally, most families play certain roles during the addiction and recovery process. See if you or a family member fits into any of these roles:

- <u>The Addict</u>: The person with the addiction is at the center. They are not necessarily the most important, however, they will be the center of attention. After all, their addiction is the issue at hand. The rest of you will assume other roles around the addict.

- <u>The Hero</u>: This is the person who feels they have to make all family members "look good" in the eyes of others. They often ignore the problem and present things in a positive light as if the problem didn't exist. The Hero is the perfectionist demanding more of The Addict than he or she can provide.

- The Mascot: The Mascot will often try to inject humor into the situation. Sometimes this humor is inappropriate and can hinder the recovery process. The Mascot is also the cheerleader providing support when possible.

- The Lost Child: This is the silent person who always seems to be in the way or left out. They are quiet and reserved not making problems. The Lost Child gives up self needs and tries to avoid conversation regarding the problem.

- The Scapegoat: This person often acts out in front of others. They divert attention from The Addict and the problems that you are all facing together.

- The Caretaker: This person is the enabler. They try to keep the whole family happy and keep all roles in balance. They often make excuses for The Addict's behavior and puts on a happy front for outsiders. The Caretaker denies that there are any problems, and usually never mention anything about addiction or recovery.

The parts played by family members lead to codependency. Members make decisions concerning what the other person needs. Codependency leads to aversion and lack of self-orientation in a situation where an addiction is present. Ultimately people "become" the part they are playing.

The goal in alcohol and drug addiction recovery is to bring each member as a whole into a situation where the problems can be dealt with. Individual talents and abilities should be integrated into the situation, allowing emotional honesty about the situation, without guilt or punishment.

People become familiar with and dependent on the role they play in families. In overcoming the family roles, you will begin to overcome issues, and what could be classified as the addiction to the role. While conquering the substance is important to the person with the addiction, a point to remember is the substance(s) is not the key to family recovery, removing the underlying roles are.

In beginning recovery, each family member must become proactive against the addiction to the role, and learn to become their true self. The goal is for each person to become independent, and then approach the substance addiction recovery as a group of individuals, rather than as people playing a part. Whole, independent people can freely contribute to the recovery of the person overcoming the addiction, while a person playing a part can only perform the role.

Each family member must realize which role they play and then start thinking about how to change that role or make it work to the advantage of The Addict. Working together is a must when it comes to getting a loved one off of drugs. Make a list of strengths and weaknesses then assess that list to see how you can use your strengths to help The Addict without bringing your weaknesses into play.

Realize that the process and that role contributes in some way toward helping. Family members should acknowledge their individual parts in this process and acknowledge that they have an integral role that is unique to them. Each person is just as important as the other.

As a family, you have to prepare to be flexible.

Overcoming drug addiction is a difficult journey – one that is met with bumps and dips and curves. Life can change from day to day even hour to hour. You need to "roll with the punches" and adapt to whatever situation is thrown at you in the whole process. As a family member, you may want to consider having an intervention.

CHAPTER 17

INTERVENTIONS

Anytime someone needs help but refuses to accept it, a family intervention is appropriate. A family intervention can be used for people engaged in any self-destructive behavior. They are especially appropriate for addicts because most understand the harm using is doing to them, but feel trapped in a vicious cycle.

Intervention is the most loving, powerful and successful method yet for helping people accept help. A family intervention can be done with love and respect in a non-confrontational, non-judgmental manner. With some, a family intervention is often the only method that will get through to them. If you have a family member that is suffering with drug or alcohol abuse, know that an intervention can be done, and it can be done now!

It certainly is not an easy decision to make when you are considering intervention for a loved one's problems. But if you are able to handle it in a loving, caring manner, you will be giving that loved one a gift that they will appreciate – eventually!

The first thing that needs to be done is have all family members and friends who might be able to make a difference agree on a time and place to meet. It's a good idea to contact a professional counselor to help you, as you may initially be apprehensive and confused. Members participating in the intervention may be conflicted about whether or not to actually do the intervention. Some may be afraid of the person; others may be angry. The goal is to move from this disorganized and chaotic state to a cohesive, focused group.

To do this, the participants meet with the leader or counselor beforehand to educate themselves about the dysfunction, to determine how to best help themselves, and to prepare for Intervention Day. This includes identifying others who should be involved, exploring appropriate treatment options, and preparing what they are going to say.

This preparation often involves several meetings,

telephone calls, and culminates in a practice session immediately prior to the Intervention Day. The time varies, but the process is usually contained within one to two weeks. Sometimes it can be shortened to a weekend.

It is important for all of you to meet prior to Intervention Day so that you can discuss what steps will be taken and how you will be approaching the person you are trying to help. Remember that you need to work together as a unit and decide what will be said beforehand.

You then need to get the person you want to help to actually show up. This can be accomplished in many ways. Use your imagination and say what you have to in order for the addicted person to arrive at the designated place.

There is no absolute right way to intervene in someone else's life. In fact, there is a school of thought that argues that any form of intervention is abhorrent, a violation of free speech and of an individual's right to choose. Nevertheless, as individuals and as a society we are always influencing others whether or not we want to, and sometimes we decide to intervene purposefully.

Intervention can be simple or it can be more

involved. The decision about what type of intervention to conduct must be up to all participating parties. A simple intervention is exactly what it sounds like. You simply ask the person you are intervening to get help for their problem. Believe it or not, sometimes this works incredibly well. Often an addict is just waiting for someone else to acknowledge their problem before they do. Once they know that everyone can see the problem, they are given permission to seek help with the support of their family and friends.

If a situation has reached dangerous proportions where a person's life is in danger, a crisis intervention is necessary. Crisis Interventions occur in dangerous situations involving reckless driving, weapons, hospital emergency rooms, or violence or threats of violence. It is obvious in these situations that a person is in immediate danger to himself or others. The immediate objective in these cases is to calm the crisis and to create safety for all. Remember, a crisis often creates golden opportunities for family members to help someone accept help.

A classical intervention requires all attention to be focused on the addict. Participants are often asked to talk with the addict and tell them what their addiction has done to them personally. It's very important to be brutally honest during these discussions. Let it all go – this is the perfect opportunity for you to get everything out. And, it may be your last.

Expect the addict to be defensive. That's normal. They will probably deny that they even have a problem at all. They may yell and scream, or try to get away. The purpose of an intervention is to get everyone's feelings out into the open, so the person you are trying to help should not be allowed to leave the room. However, avoid violence.

Be sure that your tone is sympathetic but helpful and that the person you are trying to help knows without a doubt that they have your support. Intervention can be an effective tool in the process of recovery, but it must be handled in the right way which is why we strongly suggest the help of a professional.

Your ultimate goal with an intervention is to persuade your loved one to get help with his or her addiction. If it's bad enough to warrant an intervention, you will probably want to suggest an in-patient rehabilitation center. At the very least, you should have the names and numbers of several different services they can turn to for help. Many people who want help do not know how to get help, and a long, exhaustive search can become frustrating to them.

Understand if they are insured or uninsured, so you can help them understand their options as soon as they are ready. For example, some facilities will pick them up right away, while others may require being placed on a waiting list. The more informed you are, the easier it will be for you to help. To learn your treatment options, call **1(844)775-HELP** (4357).

CHAPTER 18

THE CYCLE OF ADDICTION

Drug addiction is a chronic disease characterized by compulsive, or uncontrollable, drug seeking and use despite harmful consequences and changes in the brain, which can be long lasting. These changes in the brain can lead to the harmful behaviors seen in people who use drugs and excessively drink alcohol. Drug addiction is a Relapsing Disease, meaning those suffering often return to drug use after an attempt to stop. Relapse also occurs after years of nonuse.

The path to addiction begins with the voluntary act of taking drugs or drinking alcohol. But over time, a person's ability to choose not to do so, becomes compromised. Seeking and taking the drug becomes compulsive and involuntarily in many ways, mostly due to the effects of long-term drug exposure on brain function.

This leads to drug cravings within the brain brought on by various triggers.

Many things can "trigger" drug cravings for a recovering user. It is critical for those attempting to say clean at home, in an inpatient facility, or in prison, to learn how to recognize, avoid, and cope with triggers they are likely to be exposed to after treatment. People do not become addicted to drugs overnight. It takes continuous use occurring over a period of time, perhaps, several years, that turned into a dependence on those drugs.

Typically use begins as a means to escape. In order to stay sober, it is very important that one removes anything from their life that could "trigger" them, and cause them to want to begin using again.

Taking steps towards staying sober begins with changing your lifestyle and the people you keep in your social circles. Friends often play a big role in getting you to start using in the first place. Peer pressure is difficult to overcome, and when you are around people that use drugs, and used drugs with you in the past, your recovery is seriously compromised.

Most people hate this part of drug recovery, and fear

getting sober because of it. To stay sober, you must always keep in mind what is best for you, not necessary for anyone else. True friends will stay by your side, and may even help you stay clean. Those friends who are still struggling with addiction will keep their distance, as their drug use will be much more important to them than you are. Keep this in mind.

It is crucial to avoid situations where you may be tempted to use, especially during the initial recovery stages. For example, if you are trying to stop drinking, stay away from social situations and locations that may make it more difficult for you to not drink. That means no bars or clubs and not going to parties where alcohol is served. Think about the places where you used drugs and avoid them at all costs. Eventually, as time passes, you will become stronger and better equipped to resist the temptation to relapse.

Rehabilitation centers will have these resources readily available for you. If you chose to recover on your own, you will still need some sort of counseling to get to where you need to be in your recovery. Counseling should be seen as a requirement of your recovery. You will have very powerful forces inside your mind triggering you to want to use again. Therapy or counseling can help you stay strong against these inner demons and teach you new ways to deal with stress and anxiety that could have pushed you towards drug use in the first place.

It may help to believe in a higher power that affects your life. You will need to decide who or what that higher power we be, but please know that your recovery will be much easier if you believe in something bigger than yourself. There are countless other avenues that can help you find peace in your mind and body. You will need to discover what works best for you.

To avoid relapse, you must identify ways to make yourself much more relaxed and able to cope with the world. This will lower the probability of you feeling the need to self-medicate with drugs or alcohol. There are trained professionals that have dedicated years of their lives studying how to help you. Counselors, therapists, and Addiction Specialists are a great resource. Not only do they understand the brain and how drugs effect it, they have worked with many others in your situation.

Recovering addicts are also a great support group. It is a good idea to speak to as many as you can to stay motivated. Speaking to them should be used as a support to stay clean, but never as medical advisors. Understand that their recovery approach may not be the best for you. You should always couple your continuous recovery with help from a trained professional. They can also teach you safe and clinically tested mechanisms you can exercise on your own.

You cannot control your thoughts unless you train your mind to do so. Meditating can be a very effective way to focus, and organize your thoughts during recovery. The inner voices inside your head will be telling you all sorts of different things when you are trying to stay off drugs.

In treatment, as well as in counseling, you will be trained on how to recognize these damaging inner voices and take steps to calm them, significantly increasing your chancing of staying clean. Once mastered, your body will calm down and those voices will go away.

With time and practice, you will find yourself slipping into the state of mind you need to be in much quicker. Another good technique is to picture a relaxing place for you, and imagine you are there, feeling the sensations that the image creates in your mind. You can also use progressive muscle relaxation (PMY) to get rid of your stress, which involves concentrating on one part of the body at a time.

Exercise such as yoga or Tai Chi are also great for stress relief. Most inpatient rehabilitation facilities have fitness facilities and trainers who will teach you to concentrate on your body rather than just your mind.

Once you develop a dependence on drugs or alcohol, there will always be a temptation towards relapse in stressful situations. The coping skills you acquire during treatment will be useful to avoid relapse for the rest of your life.

CHAPTER 19
THE FOREVER FIGHT

Drug addiction is a powerful demon that can sneak up on you and take over your life before you know it has even happened. What may have started out as a recreational lifestyle can overcome one's life and effect every single aspect of it.

If you are struggling, you do not need to remain trapped in the lonely web of drug addiction. There are so many things you can do to get yourself clean and sober, and there's no better time than the present.

This book is not meant to be a specific treatment plan. It is just a guide to help get you started on the road to sobriety. We are not medical professionals. We have just brought together information and advice from some of the professional and medical organizations out there to guide you on your recovery journey.

Overcoming drug addiction is a long and often painful process. There is much that you need to know before you start, and I hope this book helped. Leading a clean lifestyle is something that is well within your reach. You now have the tools you need to go out and begin your journey towards healing yourself or aiding a loved one. Remember that a thousand-mile journey always begins with one step, and to take it one day at a time.

Getting clean is scary. Staying clean is equally as hard. Addiction Recovery is *The Forever Fight* for your life, your family, and your wellbeing. But you can do it, one day at a time!

www.ingramcontent.com/pod-product-compliance
Lightning Source LLC
Chambersburg PA
CBHW050540300426
44113CB00012B/2200

9780998921709